I KNOW
Addition & Subtraction

Brighter Child®
Carson-Dellosa Publishing LLC
Greensboro, North Carolina

Brighter Child®
Carson-Dellosa Publishing LLC
PO Box 35665
Greensboro, NC 27425 USA

ISBN 978-1-4838-4480-0

Contents

Count Ahead

Use the number line to count forward. For each problem, put your finger on the first number. Count ahead the number of spaces shown by the second number. The number you land on shows the sum. Write a number to solve each addition problem.

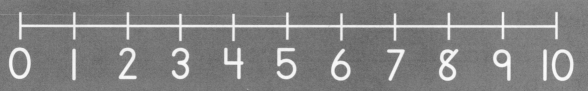

0 1 2 3 4 5 6 7 8 9 10

1 + 3 = _____	2 + 1 = _____
0 + 5 = _____	1 + 1 = _____

Count Ahead

Use the number line to count forward. Write a number to solve each addition problem.

0 1 2 3 4 5 6 7 8 9 10

$5 + 4 =$ _____

$6 + 1 =$ _____

$3 + 5 =$ _____

$2 + 8 =$ _____

Add 0

Trace and write to solve the problems.

$1 + 0 =$

$+0$

$2 + 0 =$

$3 + 0 =$

$4 + 0 =$

Draw the faces of detectives or suspects.

Add 0

Trace and write to solve the problems.

$5 + 0 =$

_____

- - - - - - -

_____

$6 + 0 =$

6

- - - - - - -

+0

$8 + 0 =$

_____

- - - - - - -

_____

$10 + 0 =$

_____

- - - - - - -

_____

Circle the badges with **0**. Draw a box around the badges with **1**.

Add 1

Trace and write to solve the problems.

| + | =

_____

- - - - - - - -

_____

2 + | =

_____

- - - - - - - -

_____

+ |

3 + | =

_____

5 + | =

_____

- - - - - - - -

_____

Circle the group with more bugs.

Add 1

Trace and write to solve the problems.

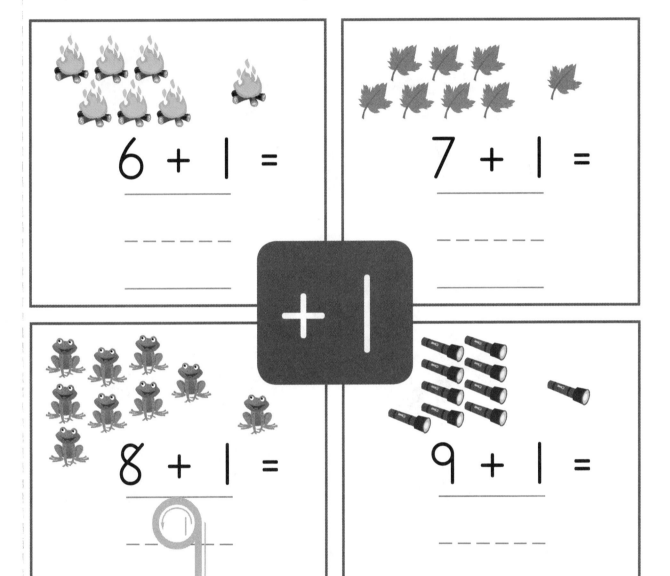

6 + 1 =

_____

- - - - - - - -

_____

7 + 1 =

_____

- - - - - - - -

_____

+ 1

8 + 1 =

9

_____

9 + 1 =

_____

- - - - - - - -

_____

Each ant has **2** eyes. How many eyes do **3** ants have altogether? Write the number.

_____

- - - - - - - -

_____

Add 2

Trace and write to solve the problems.

0 + 2 =

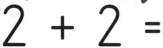

1 + 2 =

+2

2 + 2 =

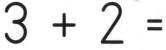

3 + 2 =

Circle the pictures that go together.

Add 2

Trace and write to solve the problems.

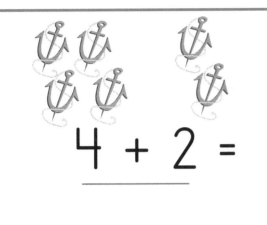

4 + 2 =

_____

_ _ _ _ _

_____

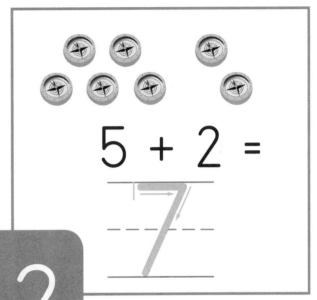

5 + 2 =

7

_ _ _ _ _

_____

+2

6 + 2 =

_ _ _ _ _

_____

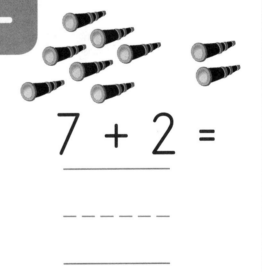

7 + 2 =

_ _ _ _ _

_____

Count the starfish. Circle the number.

0   1   2

Add 3

Trace and write to solve the problems.

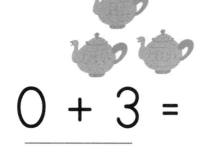

0 + 3 =

_____

- - - - -

_____

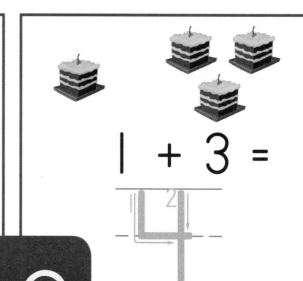

1 + 3 =

+3

2 + 3 =

- - - - -

_____

3 + 3 =

- - - - -

_____

Circle the trees that are taller. Draw an **X** on the trees that are shorter.

Add 3

Trace and write to solve the problems.

$4 + 3 =$

_____

- - - - - -

_____

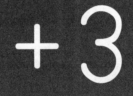

$5 + 3 =$

_____

- - - - - -

_____

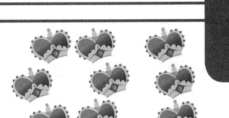

$6 + 3 =$

9

$7 + 3 =$

_____

- - - - - -

_____

Color the jewels with **2** red. Color the jewels with **3** green.

Add 4

Trace and write to solve the problems.

0 + 4 =

1 + 4 =

5

+4

2 + 4 =

3 + 4 =

Write the missing numbers.

1 _____ _____ 4

Add 4

Trace and write to solve the problems.

4 + 4 = ____

5 + 4 = ____

+4

6 + 4 = 10

Draw **4** animals. Write the number.

____

Add 5

Trace and write to solve the problems.

0 + 5 =

_____

- - - - - -

_____

1 + 5 =

- - - - - -

_____

2 + 5 = - - 7 - -

How many pairs of shoes do you see? Write the number.

_____

- - - - - -

_____

Add 5

Trace and write to solve the problems.

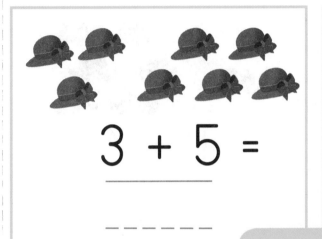

$$3 + 5 =$$

- - - - - -

_____

$$4 + 5 =$$

- - - - - -

+5

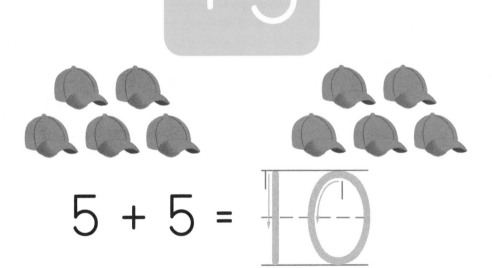

$$5 + 5 = 10$$

Circle the shirt that is different.

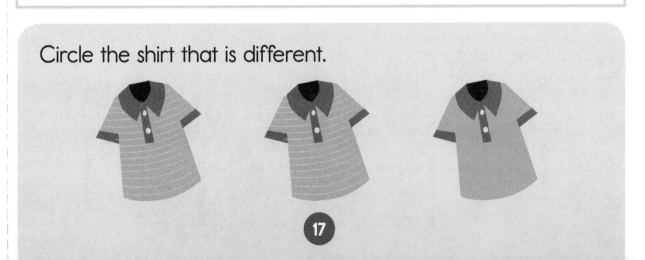

Add 6

Trace and write to solve the problems.

0 + 6 =

_____

- - - - -

_____

1 + 6 =

_____

- - - - -

_____

+6

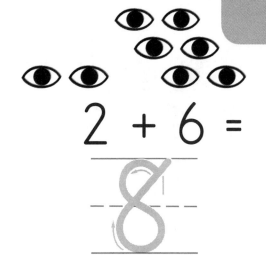

2 + 6 =

_____

8

- - - - -

_____

3 + 6 =

_____

- - - - -

_____

Circle the magnifying glasses with **6**.

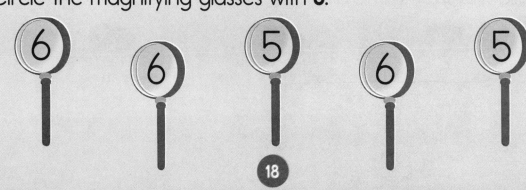

Add 7

Trace and write to solve the problems.

$$0 + 7 =$$

_____

- - - - -

_____

$$1 + 7 =$$

_____

- - - - -

_____

+7

$$2 + 7 =$$

_____

$$3 + 7 =$$

_____

- - - - -

_____

Open the safe! Circle the greatest number.

5

3   7

Add 8

Trace and write to solve the problems.

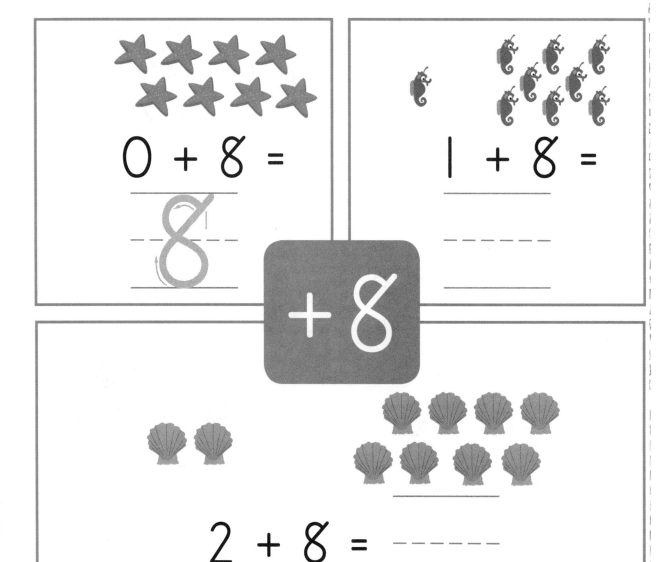

$$0 + 8 =$$

$$1 + 8 =$$

$$+8$$

$$2 + 8 =$$

Count the fish. Circle the number.

6 7 8

Add 9

Trace and write to solve the problems.

0 + 9 = _____

+9

1 + 9 = 10

Write the missing numbers.

5 ___ 7 ___ 9

Make 10

Circle the number that completes each problem.

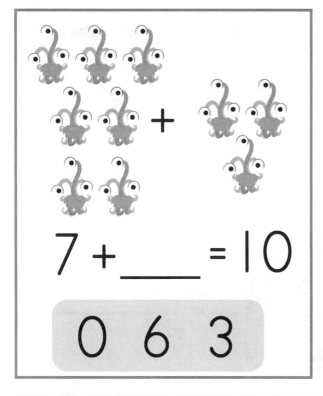

$7 + \underline{} = 10$

0   6   3

$9 + \underline{} = 10$

10   1   0

$10 + \underline{} = 10$

0   10   9

Circle the monsters that are the same.

Make 10

Circle the number that completes each problem.

$6 +$ ___ $= 10$

1   4   2

$5 +$ ___ $= 10$

4   6   5

$8 +$ ___ $= 10$

3   5   2

Draw and color 10 monster eggs. Then, write the number.

_____

_ _ _ _ _ _

_____

Make 10

Count the objects in each group. Then, draw more objects so each group has **10**.

Make 10

Count the objects in each group. Then, draw more objects so each group has **10**.

Add to 10

Trace and write to solve the problems.

$5 + 3 =$

_____

- - - - - -

_____

$8 + 1 =$

_____

- - - - - -

$6 + 4 =$

_____

- - - - - -

_____

$0 + 3 =$

3

Count the glasses of lemonade. Write the number.

_____

- - - - - -

_____

Add to 10

Trace and write to solve the problems.

7 + 2 =

_____

- - - - - -

_____

2 + 2 =

_____

- - - - - -

_____

8 + 0 =

_____

8

_____

3 + 6 =

_____

- - - - - -

_____

Draw a line to divide each sandwich into **2** equal parts.

I Know How to Add

Add. Use the pictures for help.

3
+4
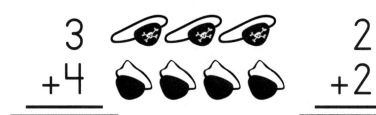
_____

2
+2

_____

- - - - - - - - - - - -

2
+3
_____

1
+7
_____

- - - - - - - - - - - -

5
+5
_____

3
+6
_____

- - - - - - - - - - - -

I Know How to Add

Add. Use the pictures for help.

4
+4
_____

3
+7
_____

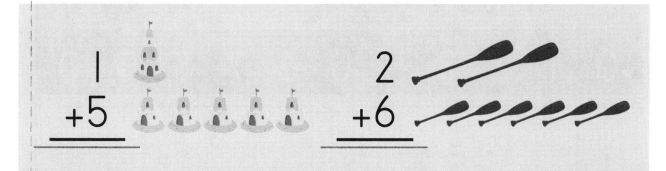

1
+5
_____

2
+6
_____

3
+3
_____

5
+3
_____

Count Back

Use the number line to count backward. For each problem, put your finger on the first number. Count back the number of spaces shown by the second number. The number you land on shows the difference. Write a number to solve each subtraction problem.

0 1 2 3 4 5 6 7 8 9 10

$2 - 1 =$ _____

$5 - 2 =$ _____

$7 - 3 =$ _____

$6 - 5 =$ _____

Count Back

Use the number line to count backward.
Write a number to solve each
subtraction problem.

| | | | | | | | | | | |
0   1   2   3   4   5   6   7   8   9   10

3 - 3 = _____

8 - 2 = _____

10 - 6 = _____

5 - 1 = _____

Subtract 0

Solve each problem. Then, trace or write the answer.

1 - 0 =

_ _ _ _ _ _

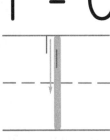

2 - 0 =

_ _ _ _ _ _

-0

3 - 0 =

_ _ _ _ _ _

5 - 0 =

_ _ _ _ _ _

Count the crabs. Circle the number.

6 7 8

© Carson-Dellosa

Subtract 0

Solve each problem. Then, trace or write the answer.

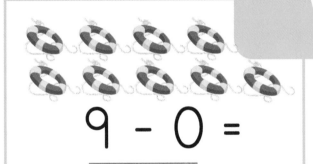

6 - 0 =

6

7 - 0 =

-0

9 - 0 =

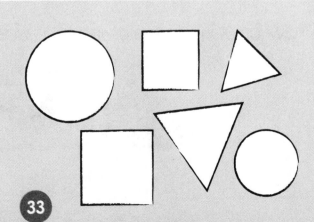

10 - 0 =

Color the circles black.
Color the squares pink.
Color the triangles green.

33

Subtract 1

Cross out an object to solve each problem. Then, trace or write the answer.

2 - 1 =

3 - 1 =

- 1

4 - 1 =

5 - 1 =

Draw an **X** on the picture that does not belong.

Subtract 1

Cross out an object to solve each problem. Then, trace or write the answer.

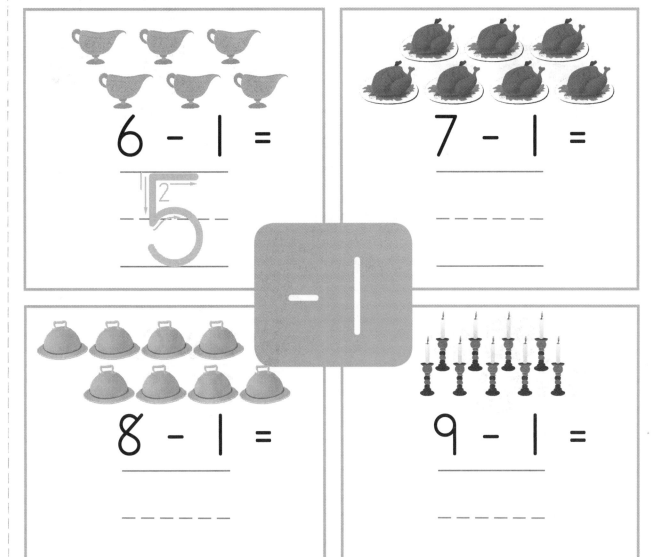

6 - 1 =

5

7 - 1 =

- 1

8 - 1 =

9 - 1 =

Count the thrones. Write the number.

Subtract 2

Cross out objects to solve each problem. Then, trace or write the answer.

$$2 - 2 =$$

----- -----

_____

$$3 - 2 =$$

----- -----

_____

$$-2$$

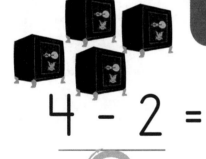

$$4 - 2 =$$

2
_____

$$5 - 2 =$$

----- -----

_____

Circle the fingerprint that is smaller. Draw an **X** on the fingerprint that is larger.

36

Subtract 2

Cross out objects to solve each problem. Then, trace or write the answer.

6 - 2 =

_____

- - - - - - -

_____

7 - 2 =

_____

- - - - - - -

_____

- 2

8 - 2 =

_____

- - - - - - -

_____

9 - 2 =

7

- - - - - - -

_____

Color **2** bats. Then, draw **2** more.

Subtract 3

Cross out objects to solve each problem. Then, trace or write the answer.

3 - 3 =

0

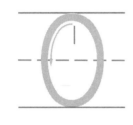

4 - 3 =

-3

5 - 3 =

6 - 3 =

Draw a monster that is shorter. Draw a monster that is taller.

Subtract 3

Cross out objects to solve each problem. Then, trace or write the answer.

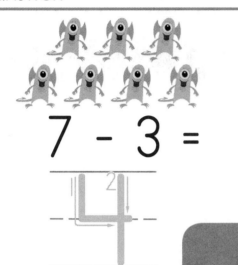

7 - 3 =

4

8 - 3 =

_ _ _ _ _ _

-3

9 - 3 =

_ _ _ _ _ _

10 - 3 =

_ _ _ _ _ _

Count the eyes on the monster. Circle the number.

2   3   4

Subtract 4

Cross out objects to solve each problem. Then, trace or write the answer.

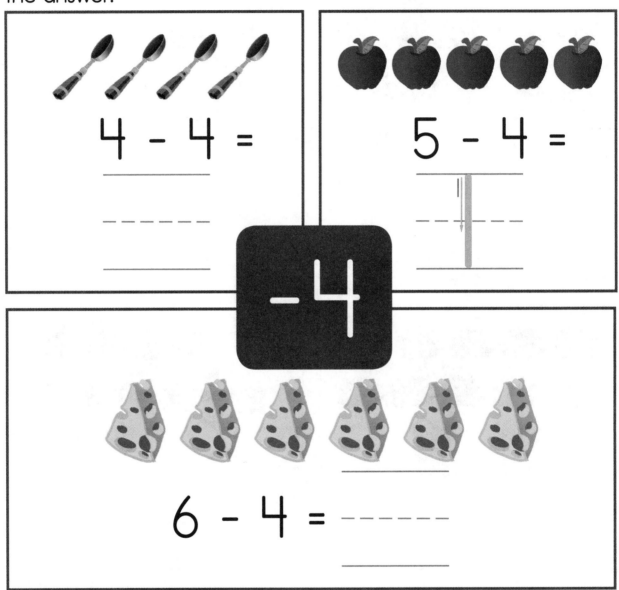

$$4 - 4 =$$

$$5 - 4 =$$

1

$$-4$$

$$6 - 4 =$$

Circle the group that has less.

40

Subtract 4

Cross out objects to solve each problem. Then, trace or write the answer.

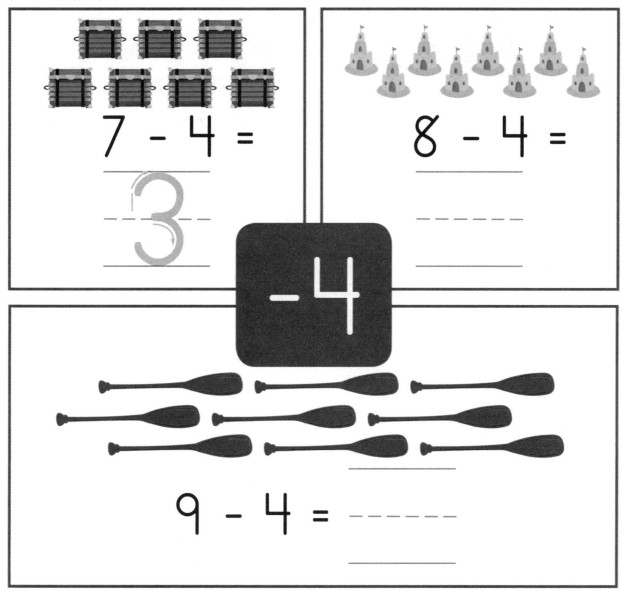

$7 - 4 =$

3

$8 - 4 =$

-4

$9 - 4 =$

Color each duck with **3** orange. Color each duck with **4** yellow.

Subtract 5

Cross out objects to solve each problem. Then, trace or write the answer.

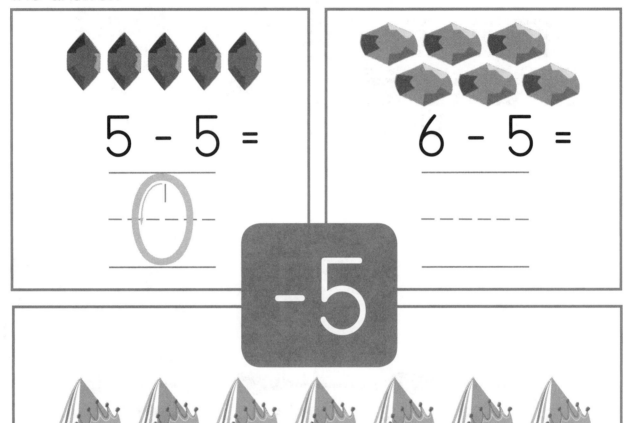

5 - 5 =

0

6 - 5 =

-5

7 - 5 =

Match the group
of cups to the
correct number.

6

8

9

Subtract 5

Cross out objects to solve each problem. Then, trace or write the answer.

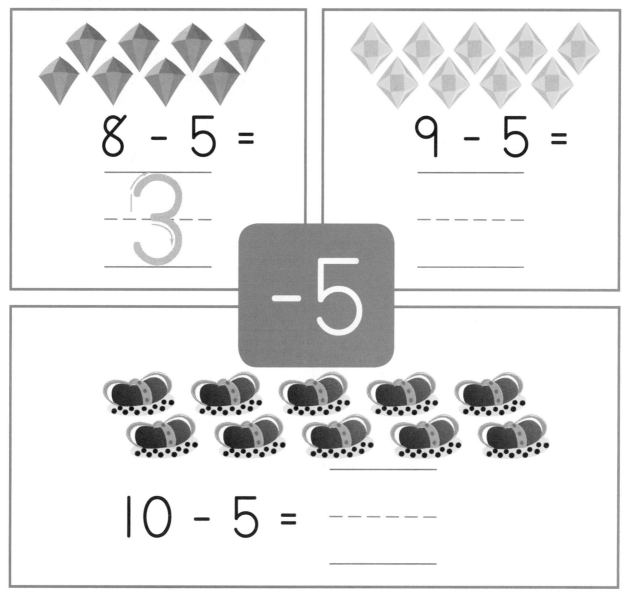

8 - 5 =

3

9 - 5 =

-5

10 - 5 =

Circle the hat that comes next.

Subtract 6

Cross out objects to solve each problem. Then, trace or write the answer.

6 - 6 =

_____

- - - - - -

_____

7 - 6 =

- - - - - -

_____

- 6

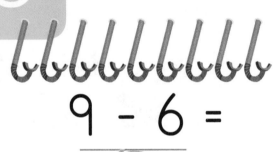

8 - 6 =

_____

- - - - - -

_____

9 - 6 =

3

Color the square blue. Color the rhombus purple.
Color the rectangle orange.

Subtract 7

Cross out objects to solve each problem. Then, trace or write the answer.

7 - 7 =

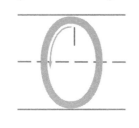

8 - 7 =

-7

9 - 7 =

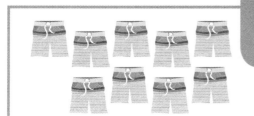

10 - 7 =

Count the palm trees. Draw an equal number of palm trees.

45

Subtract 8

Cross out objects to solve each problem. Then, trace or write the answer.

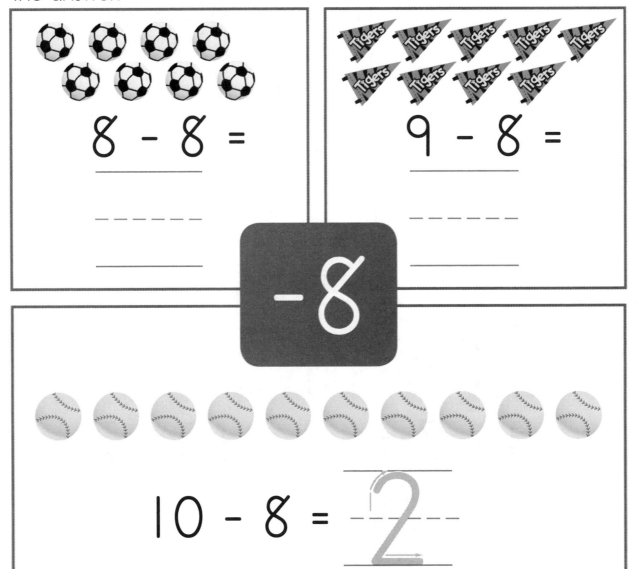

8 - 8 =

_ _ _ _ _

9 - 8 =

_ _ _ _ _

-8

10 - 8 = 2

Color the bats with **8**.

8   0   3   8

Subtract 9

Cross out objects to solve each problem. Then, trace or write the answer.

$9 - 9 =$ 0

-9

$10 - 9 =$ _____

Color the ball that comes next.

Subtract From 10

Count **10** monsters in each box. Cross out monsters to make the number shown.

9

8

6

Circle the monster that is different.

Subtract From 10

Count **10** monsters in each box. Cross out monsters to make the number shown.

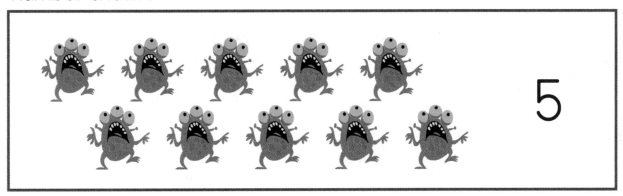

5

3

1

One monster was waiting at the bus stop. Then, two more monsters came. Draw a picture. Write and solve a problem.

Subtract Through 10

Cross out objects to solve each problem. Then, trace or write the answer.

6 – 6 =

- - - - - -
___

8 – 3 =

5
___

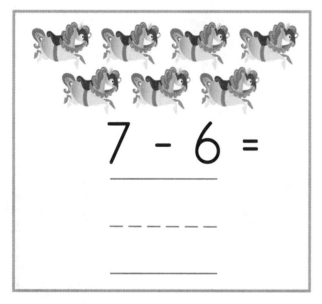

7 – 6 =

___
- - - - - -
___

5 – 4 =

___
- - - - - -
___

Circle the numbers that are less than **5**.

7   4   3   4

5   1   7   0   1

Subtract Through 10

Cross out objects to solve each problem. Then, trace or write the answer.

4 - 1 =

_____

- - - - -

_____

2 - 2 =

_____

- - - - -

_____

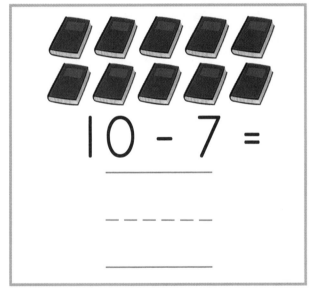

10 - 7 =

_____

- - - - -

_____

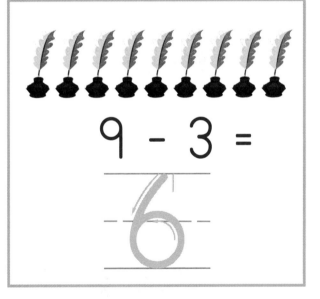

9 - 3 =

_____

6

- - - - -

On each flag, circle the number that is greater.

 6 10

 5 8

I Know How to Subtract

Subtract. Count and cross out pictures to help.

7
- 3

_ _ _ _ _

10
- 7

_ _ _ _ _

4
- 1

_ _ _ _ _

6
- 4

_ _ _ _ _

8
- 3

_ _ _ _ _

9
- 8

_ _ _ _ _

I Know How to Subtract

Subtract. Count and cross out pictures to help.

$$
\begin{array}{r} 5 \\ -2 \\ \hline \end{array}
$$

- - - - - - -

_ _ _ _ _ _ _

$$
\begin{array}{r} 10 \\ -5 \\ \hline \end{array}
$$

- - - - - - -

_ _ _ _ _ _ _

$$
\begin{array}{r} 2 \\ -0 \\ \hline \end{array}
$$

- - - - - - -

_ _ _ _ _ _ _

$$
\begin{array}{r} 7 \\ -2 \\ \hline \end{array}
$$

- - - - - - -

_ _ _ _ _ _ _

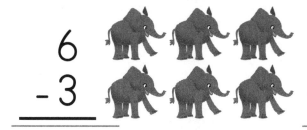

$$
\begin{array}{r} 6 \\ -3 \\ \hline \end{array}
$$

- - - - - - -

_ _ _ _ _ _ _

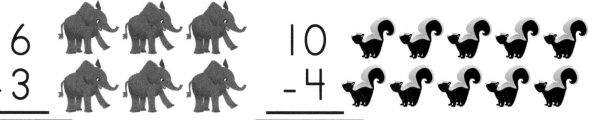

$$
\begin{array}{r} 10 \\ -4 \\ \hline \end{array}
$$

- - - - - - -

_ _ _ _ _ _ _

Add to Subtract

You can turn subtraction problems into addition problems!
Draw the missing fish. Write the missing numbers.

6 - 2 = _____

2 + [　　] = 6

7 - 4 = _____

4 + [　　] = 7

9 - 3 = _____

3 + [　　] = 9

54

Add to Subtract

You can turn subtraction problems into addition problems!
Draw the missing fish. Write the missing numbers.

$$8 - 2 = \underline{\hspace{3cm}}$$

$$5 - 1 = \underline{\hspace{3cm}}$$

$$10 - 8 = \underline{\hspace{3cm}}$$

55

Add & Subtract

Solve the problems.

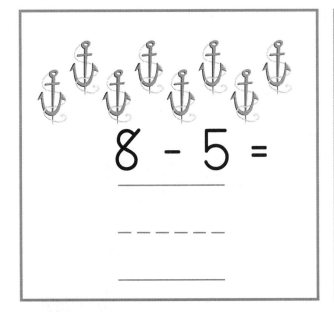

8 - 5 =

_ _ _ _ _

___

2 + 5 =

_ _ _ _ _

___

3 - 1 =

_ _ _ _ _

___

7 - 4 =

_ _ _ _ _

___

Circle the group that has less.

Add & Subtract

Solve the problems.

6 + 4 =

_ _ _ _ _ _

_____

9 - 5 =

_ _ _ _ _ _

_____

10 - 7 =

_ _ _ _ _ _

_____

5 + 4 =

_ _ _ _ _ _

_____

Draw a pirate ship!
Your drawing should
include the
shapes shown.

Add & Subtract

Solve the problems.

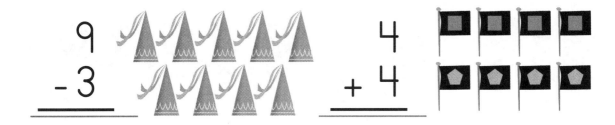

$$\begin{array}{r} 9 \\ -3 \\ \hline \end{array}$$

- - - - -

_____

$$\begin{array}{r} 4 \\ +4 \\ \hline \end{array}$$

- - - - -

_____

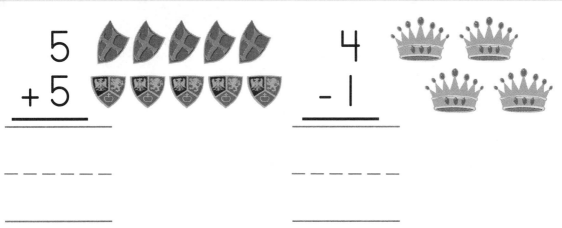

$$\begin{array}{r} 3 \\ +6 \\ \hline \end{array}$$

- - - - -

_____

$$\begin{array}{r} 10 \\ -2 \\ \hline \end{array}$$

- - - - -

_____

$$\begin{array}{r} 5 \\ +5 \\ \hline \end{array}$$

- - - - -

_____

$$\begin{array}{r} 4 \\ -1 \\ \hline \end{array}$$

- - - - -

_____

Add & Subtract

Solve the problems.

$$\begin{array}{r} 2 \\ +\ 5 \\ \hline \end{array}$$

$$\begin{array}{r} 8 \\ -\ 7 \\ \hline \end{array}$$

$$\begin{array}{r} 8 \\ +\ 2 \\ \hline \end{array}$$

$$\begin{array}{r} 5 \\ -\ 3 \\ \hline \end{array}$$

$$\begin{array}{r} 4 \\ +\ 3 \\ \hline \end{array}$$

$$\begin{array}{r} 7 \\ -\ 3 \\ \hline \end{array}$$

Word Problems

Add to solve the problems.

There are **7** 🏕 at Campground One.

There are **2** 🏕 at Campground Two.

How many 🏕 in all?

_____

_ _ _ _ _ _

_____

Aimee has **3** 👓 in her room.

She has **1** more 👓 in her beach bag.

How many 👓 in all?

_____

_ _ _ _ _ _

_____

The top shelf has **5** 📘.

The bottom shelf has **3** 📘.

How many 📘 in all?

_____

_ _ _ _ _ _

_____

Mason found **2** 🔦 with dead batteries.

He found **5** 🔦 with working batteries.

How many 🔦 did he find in all?

_____

_ _ _ _ _ _

_____

Word Problems

Add to solve the problems.

There is **1** . in the box.

Gina puts **3** more . in the box.

How many . in all?

_____

- - - - - -

_____

Robert has **0** .

He buys **9** .

How many in all?

_____

- - - - - -

_____

One pond has **4** .

Another pond has **4** .

How many in all?

_____

- - - - - -

_____

There are **3** on the table.

There are **4** in the drawer.

How many in all?

_____

- - - - - -

_____

Word Problems

Subtract to solve the problems.

There are **8** 🥚 in the cave.

Jack takes away **6** 🥚.

How many 🥚 are in the cave now?

_____

_ _ _ _ _ _

_____

10 👾 came to the party.

Then, **3** 👾 left the party.

How many 👾 are at the party now?

_____

_ _ _ _ _ _

_____

There were **9** 🍦.

The monsters ate **4** 🍦.

How many 🍦 are left?

_____

_ _ _ _ _ _

_____

There were **6** 👹 at the park.

Then, **2** 👹 left the park.

How many 👹 are at the park now?

_____

_ _ _ _ _ _

_____

62

Word Problems

Subtract to solve the problems.

There are **10** .

There are **2** .

How many more are there?

_____

- - - - - -

_____

There were **6** in the house.

Then, **1** jumped out the window.

How many were still in the house?

_____

- - - - - -

_____

There are **8** monsters with .

There are **4** monsters with .

How many more monsters have ?

_____

- - - - - -

_____

10 monsters have a pet .

4 monsters have a pet .

How many more monsters have a pet ?

_____

- - - - - -

_____

I Know How to Add & Subtract

Solve the problems. Use the code to write a letter above each problem and answer the riddle.

SECRET CODE

l = 2	e = 3	i = 5	b = 6	t = 7	N = 8	c = 9

What did the number 0 say to the number 8?

_____   _____   _____   _____

- - - - -   - - - -   - - - -   - - - -

$9 - 1$ $2 + 3$ $5 + 4$ $10 - 7$

_____   _____   _____   _____ !

- - - - -   - - - -   - - - -   - - - -

$9 - 3$ $3 + 0$ $8 - 6$ $5 + 2$